ANARCHISM AND ANARCHO-SYNDICALISM
by Rudolf Rocker

CHAPTERS

Introduction
p4

1. Ideology of Anarchism
p6

2. History of Anarchist Philosphy, From Lao-Tse to Kropotkin
p16

3. The Origins of Anarcho-Syndicalism
p24

4. Socialism and Anarcho-Syndicalism in France
p28

5. The Role of the Trade Unions: Anarcho-Syndicalist View
p31

6. The Struggle In Germany and Spain
p35

7. The Political Struggle: Anarcho-Syndicalist View
p37

8. Anarcho-Syndicalism Since the First World War
p41

Published by
FREEDOM PRESS
84b Whitechapel High Street, London E1 7QX and
NORTH LONDON SOLIDARITY FEDERATION

www.freedom press.org.uk

www.solfed.org.uk

Printed 1973, 1988, 2001, this edition with a new introduction in 2013

ISBN 978-1-904491-22-4

This essay was first published in the American publication *European Ideologies* and in 1960 was included in the Freedom Press and Libertarian Bookclub editions of Eltzbacher's *Anarchism*

Printed by print24

1

ABOUT THE AUTHOR
by Rob Ray

Born into a left-wing family in Mainz, Germany on March 25 1873, Johann Rudolf Rocker lost his father Georg Philipp at the age of four and was initially raised by his mother, Anna Margaretha.

Having initially relied on the support of her extended family to provide for Rocker and his two siblings, Margaretha married bookbinder Ludwig Baumgartner in 1884, but the marriage was to last only three years and she died of cancer in 1887.

Rocker, then aged 14, was moved into an orphanage after Baumgartner found a new partner but despised his surroundings and repeatedly escaped, managing to hide for six months working on a trawler before finally being returned.

He would later credit the institution's efficient but uncaring approach as the inspiration for his political journey towards anarchism.

Heavily influenced by his uncle Carl Naumann, a Social Democratic Party (SDP) member and bookbinder with a passion for learning, Rocker himself apprenticed in the trade and joined the SDP while devouring Naumann's extensive library.

However his politics shifted far to the left of his mentor's and he joined an anarchist-inspired internal faction of SDP, The Youth, which was quickly expelled.

Now 17, Rocker began to travel widely following his trade and political interests, visiting Brussels for the Second International in 1891 and beginning to write for anarchist publications in 1892 – an activity which coincided with police harassment which forced him to move to Paris for two years.

In 1895 Rocker was stranded in London as he fought to avoid military service, taking lodgings in the German exile enclave on Carburton Street and immersing himself in the anarchist-leaning sphere.

He quickly grew disillusioned with the infighting of the German scene however as he was accused first of theft and then of spying and cleared in both cases – it seems likely he was the victim of attempts to dislodge him from influential roles.

In 1897 he moved to Hanbury Street as he grew closer to the Jewish socialist community, and met his lifelong partner Milly Witkop (1877-1953), a Ukranian immigrant and radical whose earnest intensity was said to be a perfect match for his ebullient personality.

Introduction

A prolific writer and agitator, Witkop would co-edit a number of publications with Rocker while also independently acting as a key figure in the founding of women's unions in Germany through the 1920s in response to a failure to tackle sexism in industry by the anarcho-syndicalist FAUD union.

Rocker, a gifted linguist, learned Yiddish and along with Witkop co-edited what were to become two of the biggest anarchist papers in London, Arbeter Fraint and Germinal.

Most notably he and Witkop agitated to improve the Jewish trade unions and were leading organisers in the pivotal tailors' strike during the Great Unrest of 1912, helping to dismantle sweatshop labour in London's East End.

During this time he also began to lecture and briefly helped to run an anarchist bureau to try and co-ordinate the then rapidly expanding syndicalist unions of Europe.

However their publications were shut down and the Jewish anarchist movement broken as World War I began. Rocker's anti-war agitation saw him jailed as a German POW before his deportation in 1918.

Returning to Germany, he immediately helped found FAUD and become a key agitator against anarchist involvement with the newly-minted USSR, warning that Russia's Communist Party would be even worse than the monarchy it had overthrown. Instead he argued for the founding of an anarchist international and in 1922 helped set up the International Working Men's Association as its general secretary.

That year would mark the high point of anarchism in his lifetime. The next decade would be characterised by bitterness and failure as FAUD, outflanked by the better-organised social democrats, collapsed from 150,000 to 4,000 members before being wiped out by the Nazi government in the run-up to World War II.

Forced to flee in 1933, Rocker and Witkop settled in New York where they became well-known figures, and Rocker tried to document and explain his experiences through 40 years at the heart of European anarchism.

In 1937, Rocker wrote Anarcho-Syndicalism, which remains one of the best sources of information about that period available today. This abridged version, aimed at offering a more accessible introduction and history, was written in 1948.

Rudolf Rocker died on September 19th, 1958.

1. IDEOLOGY OF ANARCHISM

Anarchism is a definite intellectual current of social thought, whose adherents advocate the abolition of economic monopolies and of all political and social coercive institutions within society. In place of the capitalist economic order,

Anarchists would have a free association of all productive forces based upon co-operative labour, which would have for its sole purpose the satisfying of the necessary requirements of every member of society. In place of the present national states with their lifeless machinery of political and bureaucratic institutions, anarchists desire a federation of free communities which shall be bound to one another by their common economic and social interests and arrange their affairs by mutual agreement and free contract.

Anyone who studies profoundly the economic and political development of the present social system will recognise that these objectives do not spring from the utopian ideas of a few imaginative innovators, but that they are the logical outcome of a thorough examination of existing social maladjustments, which, with every new phase of the present social conditions, manifest themselves more plainly and more unwholesomely. Modern monopoly capitalism and the totalitarian state are merely the last stages in a development which could culminate in no other end.

The portentous development of our present economic system, leading to a mighty accumulation of social wealth in the hands of privileged minorities and to a constant repression of the great masses of the people, prepared the way for the present political and social reaction and befriended it in every way. It sacrificed the general interests of human society to the private interests of individuals, and thus systematically undermined a true relationship between men.

People forgot that industry is not an end in itself, but should be only a means to insure to man his material subsistence and to make accessible to him the blessings of a higher intellectual culture. Where industry is everything, where labour loses its ethical importance and man is nothing, there begins the realm of ruthless economic despotism whose workings are no less disastrous than those of any political despotism. The two mutually augment one another; they are fed from the same source.

Our modern social system has internally split the social organism of every country into hostile classes, and externally it has broken up the common cultural circle into hostile nations; both classes and nations confront one another with open antagonism, and by their ceaseless warfare keep the communal social life in continual convulsions.

Two world wars within half a century and their terrible after-effects, and the constant danger of new wars, which today dominates all peoples, are only the logical consequences of this unendurable condition which can only lead to further universal catastrophes. The mere fact that most states are obliged today to spend the better part of their annual income for so-called national defence and the liquidation of old war debts is proof of the untenability of the present status; it should make clear to everybody that the alleged protection which the state affords the individual is certainly purchased too dearly.

The ever-growing power of a soulless political bureaucracy which supervises and safeguards the life of man from the cradle to the grave is putting ever-greater obstacles in the way of co-operation among human beings.

A system which in every act of its life sacrifices the welfare of large sections of the people, of whole nations. to the selfish lust for power and the economic interests of small minorities must necessarily dissolve the social ties and lead to a constant war of each against all. This system has merely been the pacemaker for the great intellectual and social reaction which finds its expression today in modern fascism and the idea of the totalitarian state. far surpassing the obsession for power of the absolute monarchy of past centuries and seeking to bring every sphere of human activity under the control of the state.

"All for the state; all through the state; nothing without the state!" became the leitmotiv of a new political theology which has its various systems of ecclesiastical theology God is everything and man nothing, so for this modern political creed the state is everything and the citizen nothing.

And just as the words the "will of God" were used to justify the will of privileged castes, so today there hides behind the will of the state only the selfish interests of those who feel called upon to interpret

1. Jean-Jacques Rousseau (1712-1778) was a key romanticist and one of the original designers of the "social contract" theory of liberalism where political elites derive their authority from the consent of the individuals they govern

this will in their own sense and to force it upon the people.

In modern anarchism we have the confluence of the two great currents which before and since the French Revolution have found such characteristic expression in the intellectual life of Europe: socialism and liberalism.

Modern socialism developed when profound observers of social life came to see more and more dearly that political constitutions and changes in the form of government could never get to the root of the great problem that we call the social question. Its supporters recognised that an equalising of social and economic conditions for the benefit of all, despite the loveliest of theoretical assumptions. is not possible as long as people are separated into classes on the basis of their owning or not owning property, classes whose mere existence excludes in advance any thought of a genuine community.

And so there developed the conviction that only by the elimination of economic monopolies and by common ownership of the means of production does a condition of social justice become feasible, a condition in which society shall become a real community, and human labour shall no longer serve the ends of exploitation but assure the wellbeing of everyone.

But as soon as socialism began to assemble its forces and become a movement, there at once came to light certain differences of opinion due to the influence of the social environment in different countries. It is a fact that every political concept from theocracy to Caesarism and dictatorship have affected certain factions of the socialist movement.

Meanwhile, two other great currents in political thought, had a decisive significance on the development of socialist ideas: liberalism, which had powerfully stimulated advanced minds in the Anglo-Saxon countries, Holland and Spain in particular, and democracy, in the sense to which Rousseau[1] gave expression in his *Social Contract*, and which found its most influential representatives in the leaders of French Jacobinism.

While liberalism in its social theories started off from the individual and wished to limit the state's activities to a minimum, democracy took its stand on an abstract collective concept, Rousseau's general will, which it sought to fix in the national state. liberalism and democracy were pre-eminently political concepts, and since most of the original adherents of both did scarcely consider the economic conditions of society, the further development of these conditions could not be practically reconciled with the original principles of democracy, and still less with those of liberalism.

Democracy with its motto of equality of all citizens before the law, and liberalism with its right of man over his own person, both were wrecked on the realities of capitalist economy. As long as millions of human beings in every country have to sell their labour to a small minority of owners, and sink into the most wretched misery if they can find no buyers, the so-called equality before the law remains merely a pious fraud, since the laws are made by those who find themselves in possession of the social wealth. But in the same way there can be no talk of a right over one's own person, for that right ends when one is compelled to submit to the economic dictation of another if one does not want to starve.

In common with liberalism, anarchism represents the idea that the happiness and prosperity of the individual must be the standard in all social matters. And, in common with the great representatives of liberal thought, it has also the idea of limiting the functions of government to a minimum. Its adherents have followed this thought to its ultimate consequences, and wish to eliminate every institution of political power from the life of society. When Jefferson[2] clothes the basic concept of liberalism in the words: "That government is best which governs least," then anarchists say with Thoreau[3]: "That government is best which governs not at all."

In common with the founders of socialism, anarchists demand the abolition of economic monopoly in every form and shape and uphold common ownership of the soil and all other means of production, the use of which must be available to all without distinction; for personal and social freedom is conceivable only on the basis of equal economic conditions for everybody.

Within the socialist movement itself the anarchists represent the viewpoint that the struggle against capitalism must be at the same time a struggle against all coercive institutions of political power, for in history economic exploitation has always gone hand in hand with political and social oppression.

The exploitation of man by man and the domination of man over man are inseparable, and each is the condition of the other.

2. Thomas Jefferson (1743-1846) was a US president and founding father who championed equal political rights (for men) against those of the aristocracy

3. Henry Thoreau (1817–1862) was an influential early advocate of the idea that the individual should use civil disobedience to curb an immoral state

1. Karl Marx (1818-1883), remains a key theoretician for left wingers, Leninists and anarchists alike. His work Das Kapital is considered one of the great critiques of capitalism. His proposed solutions however drove a wedge between him and the anarchists of the time (see notes, p19 and 24)

As long as a possessing and a non-possessing group of human beings face one another in enmity within society, the state will be indispensable to the possessing minority for the protection of its privileges. When this condition of social injustice vanishes to give place to a higher order of things, which shall recognise no special rights and shall have as its basic assumption the community of social interests, government over men must yield the field to the administration of economic and social affairs, or, to speak with Saint Simon: "The time will come when the art of governing men will disappear. A new art will take its place, the art of administering things." In this respect anarchism has to be regarded as a kind of voluntary socialism.

This disposes also of the theory maintained by Marx[1] and his followers that the state, in the form of a proletarian dictatorship, is a necessary transitional stage to a classless society, in which the state, after the elimination of all class conflicts and then the classes themselves, will dissolve itself and vanish from the canvas.

For this concept, which completely mistakes the real nature of the state and the significance in history of the factor of political power, is only the logical outcome of so-called economic materialism, which sees in all the phenomena of history merely the inevitable effects of the methods of production of the time. Under the influence of this theory people came to regard the different forms of the state and all other social institutions as a "juridical and political superstructure on the economic edifice" of society, and thought that they had found in it the key to every historic process. In reality every section of history affords us thousands of examples of the way in which the economic development of countries was set back for centuries by the state and its power policy.

Before the rise of the ecclesiastical monarchy, Spain, industrially, was the most advanced country in Europe and held the first place in economic production in almost every field. But a century after the triumph of the Christian monarchy most of its industries had disappeared; what was left of them survived only in the most wretched condition. In most industries they had reverted to the most primitive methods of production.

Agriculture collapsed, canals and waterways fell into ruin, and vast stretches of the country were transformed into deserts. Princely absolutism in

Europe, with its silly "economic ordinances" and "Industrial Legislation," which severely punished any deviation from the prescribed methods of production and permitted no new inventions, blocked industrial progress in European countries for centuries, and prevented its natural development. And even now after the horrible experiences of two world wars, the power policy of the larger national states proves to be the greatest obstacle to the reconstruction of European economy,

In Russia, however, where the so-called dictatorship of the proletariat has ripened into reality, the aspirations of a particular party for political power have prevented any truly socialistic reorganisation of economic life and have forced the country into the slavery of a grinding state-capitalism.

The proletarian dictatorship, which naive souls believe is an inevitable transition stage to real socialism, has to-day grown into a frightful despotism and a new imperialism, which lags behind the tyranny of fascist states in nothing. The assertion that the state must continue to exist until society is no longer divided into hostile classes almost sounds in the light of all historical experience, like a bad joke.

Every type of political power presupposes some particular form of human slavery, for the maintenance of which it is called into being. Just as outwardly, that is, in relation to other states the state has to create certain artificial antagonisms in order to justify its existence, so also internally the cleavage of society into castes, ranks and classes is an essential condition of its continuance. The development of the Bolshevist bureaucracy in Russia under the alleged dictatorship of the proletariat – which has never been anything but the dictatorship of a small clique over the proletariat and the whole Russian people is merely a new instance of an old historical experience which has repeated itself countless times.

This new ruling class, which today is rapidly growing into a new aristocracy, is set apart from the great masses of the Russian peasants and workers just as clearly as are the privileged castes and classes in other countries from the mass of the people. And this situation becomes still more unbearable when a despotic state denies to the lower classes the right to complain of existing conditions, so that any protest is made at the risk of their lives.

1. Pierre-Joseph Proudhon (1809-1865) is widely regarded as one of the key figures of anarchism and the first to declare himself an anarchist. Famously he declared laws "spider webs for the rich and mighty, steel chains for the poor and weak, fishing nets in the hands of government." His most noted work was *What Is Property?*

But even a far greater degree of economic equality than that which exists in Russia would be no guarantee against political and social oppression. Economic equality alone is not social liberation. It is precisely this which all the schools of authoritarian socialism have never understood. In the prison, in the cloister, or in the barracks one finds a fairly high degree of economic equality, as all the inmates are provided with the same dwelling, the same food, the same uniform, and the same tasks.

The ancient Inca state in Peru and the Jesuit state in Paraguay had brought equal economic provision for every inhabitant to a fixed system, but in spite of this the vilest despotism prevailed there, and the human being was merely the automaton of a higher will on whose decisions he had not the slightest influence. It was not without reason that Proudhon[1] saw in a "socialism" without freedom the worst form of slavery.

The urge for social justice can only develop properly and be effective when it grows out of man's sense of freedom and responsibility, and is based upon it. In other words, socialism will be free or it will not be at all. In its recognition of this fact lies the genuine and profound justification of anarchism.

Institutions serve the same purpose in the life of society as physical organs do in plants and animals; they are the organs of the social body. Organs do not develop arbitrarily, but owe their origin to definite necessities of the physical and social environment. Changed conditions of life produce changed organs. But an organ always performs the function it was evolved to perform, or a related one. And it gradually disappears or becomes rudimentary as soon as its function is no longer necessary to the organism.

The same is true of social institutions. They, too, do not arise arbitrarily, but are called into being by special social needs to serve definite purposes. In this way the modern state was evolved, after economic privileges and class divisions associated with them had begun to make themselves more and more conspicuous in the framework of the old social order.

The newly-arisen possessing classes had need of a political instrument of power to maintain their economic and social privileges over the masses of their own people, and to impose them from without on other groups of human beings.

Thus arose the appropriate social conditions for the evolution of the modern state as the organ of political power for the forcible subjugation and oppression of the non-possessing classes. This task is the essential reason for its existence. Its external forms have altered in the course of its historical development, but its functions have always remained the same. They have even constantly broadened in just the measure in which its supporters have succeeded in making further fields of social activities subservient to their ends.

And, just as the functions of a physical organ cannot be arbitrarily altered so that, for example, one cannot, at will, hear with one's eyes or see with one's ears, so also one cannot, at pleasure, transform an organ of social oppression into an instrument for the liberation of the oppressed.

Anarchism is no patent solution for all human problems, no Utopia of a perfect social order (as it has so often been called), since, on principle, it rejects all absolute schemes and concepts. It does not believe in any absolute truth, or in any definite final goals for human development, but in an unlimited perfectibility of social patterns and human living conditions which are always straining after higher forms of expression, and to which, for this reason, one cannot assign any definite terminus nor set any fixed goal.

The greatest evil of any form of power is just that it always tries to force the rich diversity of social life into definite forms and adjust it to particular norms. The stronger its supporters feel themselves, the more completely they succeed in bringing every field of social life into their service, the more crippling is their influence on the operation of all creative cultural forces, the more unwholesomely does it affect the intellectual and social development of power and a dire omen for our times, for it shows with frightful clarity to what a monstrosity Hobbes' Leviathan[2] can be developed. It is the perfect triumph of the political machine over mind and body, the rationalisation of human thought, feeling and behaviour according to the established rules of the officials and, consequently, the end of all true intellectual culture.

Anarchism recognises only the relative significance of ideas, institutions, and social conditions. It is, therefore not a fixed, self enclosed social system, but rather a definite trend in the historical development of mankind, which, in contrast with the intellectual guardianship of all clerical and governmental institutions, strives for

2. *Leviathan* by Thomas Hobbes was published in 1651 and argued that a form of social contract overseen by an absolute monarch and a harsh central government was the only way to avoid chaos. Ironically he was eventually banned from writing altogether in 1666 by a harsh, royalist government

1. Friedrich Nietzsche (1844-1900) espoused a form of individualism that significantly inspired nihilism, existentialism and more recently, post-modernism. His ideal of a race of people operating above and beyond the morality of normal humans to rebuild the world in their image turned out to be somewhat problematic in practice

the free unhindered unfolding of all the individual and social forces in life. Even freedom is only a relative, not an absolute concept, since it tends constantly to broaden its scope and to affect wider circles in manifold ways.

For the anarchist, freedom is not an abstract philosophical concept, but the vital concrete possibility for every human being to bring to full development all capacities and talents with which nature has endowed him, and turn them to social account. The less this natural development of man is interfered with by ecclesiastical or political guardianship, the more efficient and harmonious will human personality become, the more will it become the measure of the intellectual culture of the society in which it has grown. This is the reason why all great culture periods in history have been periods of political weakness, for political systems are always set upon the mechanising and not the organic development of social forces. State and Culture are irreconcilable opposites.

Nietzsche[1], who was not an anarchist, recognised this very clearly when he wrote:

"No-one can finally spend more than he has. That holds good for individuals; it holds good for peoples. If one spends oneself for power, for higher politics, for husbandry, for commerce, parliamentarism, military interests – if one gives away that amount of reason, earnestness, will, self-mastery which constitutes one's real self for one thing, he will not have it for the other.

"Culture and the state – let no one be deceived about this – are antagonists: the Culture State is merely a modern idea. The one lives on the other, the one prospers at the expense of the other. All great periods of culture are periods of political decline. Whatever is great in a cultured sense is non-political, is even anti-political."

Where the influence of political power on the creative forces in society is reduced to a minimum, there culture thrives the best, for political rulership always strives for uniformity and tends to subject every aspect of social life to its guardianship. And, in this, it finds itself in unescapable contradiction to the creative aspirations of cultural development, which is always on the quest for new forms and fields of social activity, and for which freedom of expression, the many-sidedness and the continual changing of things, are just as vitally necessary as rigid forms, dead rules, and the forcible suppression of ideas are for the conservation of political power.

Every successful piece of work stirs the desire for greater perfection and deeper inspiration; each new form becomes the herald of new possibilities of development. But power always tries to keep things as they are, safely anchored to stereotypes. That has been the reason for all revolutions in history. Power operates only destructively, bent always on forcing every manifestation of social life into the straitjacket of its rules. Its intellectual expression is dead dogma, its physical form brute force. And this unintelligence of its objectives sets its stamp on its representatives also, and renders them often stupid and brutal, even when they were originally endowed with the best talents. One who is constantly striving to force everything into a mechanical order at last becomes a machine himself and loses all human feelings.

It was from this understanding that modern anarchism was born and draws its moral force. Only freedom can inspire men to great things and bring about intellectual and social transformations. The art of ruling men has never been the art of educating and inspiring them to a new shaping of their lives.

Dreary compulsion has at its command only lifeless drill, which smothers any vital initiative at its birth and brings forth only subjects, not free men. Freedom is the very essence of life, the impelling force in all intellectual and social development, the creator of every new outlook for the future of mankind. The liberation of man from economic exploitation and from intellectual, social and political oppression, which finds its highest expression in the philosophy of anarchism, is the first prerequisite for the evolution of a higher social culture and a new humanity.

Sidebar notes:

1. Lao-Tse (b604BC), founder of Taoism

2. Carpocrates (b100sBC) rejected the churches' morality

3. Chel ický (b1390) argued that seeking power was a sin

4. Leo Tolstoy (b1828), Russian Christian anarchist

5. François Rabelais (b1494), French satirist of the elite

6. Étienne de La Boétie (b1530), key critic of tyranny

7. Maréchal (b1530), scathing political essayist

8. Denis Diderot (b1731) helped lead the Enlightenment

9. Godwin (b1756), first modern anarchist thinker in England

10. Buchanan (b1506), Scottish proponent of "power to the people"

11. Hooker (b1554), a founder of Anglicanism and attacked concept of divine right

12. Winstanley (1609), leading Leveller

2. HISTORY OF ANARCHIST PHILOSPHY, FROM LAO-TSE TO KROPOTKIN

Anarchist ideas are to be found in almost every period of known history. We encounter them in the Chinese sage, Lao-Tse[1] (The Course and The Right Way), and the later Greek philosophers, the Hedonists and Cynics and other advocates of so-called natural right, and particularly, in Zeno, the founder of the Stoic school and opposer of Plato.

They found expression in the teachings of the Gnostic Carpocrates[2] in Alexandria, and had an unmistakable influence on certain Christian sects of the Middle Ages in France, Germany, Italy, Holland and England, most of which fell victims to the most savage persecutions.

In the history of the Bohemian Reformation they found a powerful champion in Peter Chelcicky[3], who in his work, *The Net of Faith*, passed the same judgment on the Church and the State as Tolstoy[4] did centuries later.

Among the great Humanists there was Rabelais[5], who in his description of the happy Abbey of Theleme (Gargantua) presented a picture of life freed from all authoritarian restraints. Of other pioneers of libertarian thinking we will mention here only La Boetie[6], Sylvain Marechal[7], and, above all, Diderot[8], in whose voluminous writings one finds thickly strewn the utterances of a really great mind which had rid itself of every authoritarian prejudice.

Meanwhile, it was reserved for more recent history to give a clear form to the anarchist conception of life and to connect it with the immediate process of social evolution.

This was done for the first time by William Godwin[9] in his splendidly conceived work, *An Enquiry Concerning Political Justice and its Influence upon General Virtue and Happiness* (London, 1793). Godwin's work was, we might say, the ripened fruit of that long evolution of the concepts of political and social radicalism in England which proceeds from George Buchanan[10] through Richard Hooker[11], Gerard Winstanley[12], Algernon Sidney[13], John Locke[14], Robert Wallace[15] and John Bellers[16] to Jeremy Bentham[17], Joseph Priestley[18], Richard Price[19] and Thomas Paine[20].

Godwin recognised very clearly that the cause of social evils is to be sought, not in the form of the state, but in its very existence. But he also recognised that human beings can only live together naturally and freely when the proper economic conditions for this are given, and the individual is no longer subject to exploitation by others, a consideration which most of the representatives of mere political radicalism almost wholly overlooked. Hence they were later compelled to make constantly greater concessions to the state which they had wished to restrict to a minimum.

Godwin's idea of a stateless society assumed the social ownership of the land and the instruments of labour and the carrying on of economic life by free co-operatives of producers. Godwin's work had a strong influence on advanced circles of the English workers and the more enlightened sections of the liberal intelligentsia.

Most important of all, he contributed to the young socialist movement in England, which found its maturest exponents in Robert Owen[21], John Gray[22] and William Thompson[23], that unmistakably libertarian character which it had for a long time, and which it never assumed in Germany and many other countries.

Also the French socialist Charles Fourier[24], with his theory of attractive labour must be mentioned, here as one of the pioneers of libertarian ideas.

But a far greater influence on the development of anarchist theory was that of Pierre Joseph Proudhon (1809-1865), one of the most gifted and certainly the most many-sided writer of modern socialism.

Proudhon was completely rooted in the intellectual and social life of his period, and these influenced his attitude upon every question with which he dealt. Therefore he is not to be judged, as he has been even by many of his later followers, by his special practical proposals, which were born of the needs of the hour.

Among the numerous socialist thinkers of his time he was the one who understood most profoundly the cause of social maladjustment, and possessed, besides, the greatest breadth of vision.

He was the outspoken opponent of all artificial social systems, and saw in social evolution the eternal urge to new and higher forms of intellectual and social life; it was his conviction that this evolution could not be bound by any definite abstract formulas.

13. Sidney (b1623), well-known Republican

14. Locke (b1632) 'the father of classical liberalism'

15. Rocker may be referring to the preacher and economist (b1697)

16. Bellers (b1654), Quaker and educationalist

17. Bentham (b1748), leading utilitarian theorist.

18. Priestly (b1733), famed defender of dissent

19. Price (b1723), Welsh Dissenter and feminist

20. US founding father Paine (b1737) wrrote *The Rights of Man*

21. Owen (b1771), key co-operativist and atheist

22. Gray (b1799), early ally of "one bank" economics

23. Thompson (b1775), major influence on Marx

24. Fourier (b1772), French utopian socialist

1. Giuseppe Mazzini (b1805), the first man to define and epitomise modern nationalism

2. Giuseppe Garibaldi (b1807), leading figure in the unification of Italy and collaborator of Mazzini's

3. Joachim Lelewel (b1786), Polish nationalist historian

4. Warren (b1798) was the first US individualist anarchist

5. Pearl Andrews (b1812) followed Warren into the arena and coined the "just wage" theory

6. Greene (b1819), advocate of free banking

7. Spooner (b1808), leading abolitionist and individualist

Proudhon opposed the influence of the Jacobin tradition, which dominated the thinking of the French democrats and most of the socialists of that period, with the same determination as the interference of the central state and economic monopoly in the natural progress of social advance. To him ridding society of those two cancerous growths was the great task of the nineteenth century revolution.

Proudhon was not a communist. He condemned property as merely the privilege of exploitation, but he recognised the ownership of the instruments of labour for all, made effective through industrial groups bound to one another by free contract, so long as this right was not made to serve the exploitation of others and as long as the full product of his individual labour was assured to every member of society.

This association based on reciprocity (mutuality) guarantees the enjoyment of equal rights by each in exchange for social services. The average working time required for the completion of any product becomes the measure of its value and is the basis of mutual exchange by labour notes. In this way capital is deprived of its usurial power and is completely bound up with the performance of work. Being made available to all it ceases to be an instrument for exploitation.

Such a form of economy makes any political coercive apparatus superfluous. Society becomes a league of free communities which arrange their affairs according to need. by themselves or in association with others, and in which man's freedom is the equal freedom of others not its limitation, but its security and confirmation. "The freer, the more independent and enterprising the individual is the better for society."

This organisation of federalism in which Proudhon saw the immediate future of mankind sets no definite limitations on future possibilities of development and offers the widest scope to every individual and social activity. Starting out from the point of federation, Proudhon combated likewise the aspiration for political and national unity of the awakening nationalism of the time which found such strong advocates in Mazzini[1], Garibaldi[2], Lelewel[3] and others. In this respect he recognised more clearly the real nature of nationalism than most of his contemporaries. Proudhon exerted a strong influence on the development of socialism, which made itself felt especially in the Latin countries.

Ideas similar to the economic and political conceptions of Proudhon were propagated by the followers of so-called individualist anarchism in America which found able exponents in such men as Josiah Warren[4], Stephen Pearl Andrews[5], William B. Greene[6], Lysander Spooner[7], Benjamin R. Tucker[8], Ezra Heywood[9], Francis D. Tandy[10] and many others, though none of them could approach Proudhon's breadth of view.

Characteristic of this school of libertarian thought is the fact that most of its representatives took their political ideas not from Proudhon but from the traditions of American liberalism, so that Tucker could assert that "anarchists are merely consistent Jeffersonian democrats".

A unique expression of libertarian ideas is to be found in Max Stirner's[11] (1806-1856) book, *Der Einzige und sein Eigentum*, which, it is true, passed quickly into oblivion and had no influence on the development of the anarchist movement as such. Stirner's book is predominantly a philosophic work which traces man's dependence on so-called higher powers through all its devious ways, and is not timid about drawing inferences from the knowledge gained by the survey. It is the book of a conscious and deliberate insurgent, which reveals no reverence for any authority, however exalted. and, therefore appeals powerfully to independent thinking.

Anarchism found a virile champion of vigorous revolutionary energy in Michael A. Bakunin[12], who based his ideas upon the teachings of Proudhon, but extended them on the economic side when he, along with the federalist wing of the First International, advocated collective ownership of the land and all other means of production, and wished to restrict the right of private property only to the product of individual labour.

Bakunin also was an opponent of communism, which in his time had a thoroughly authoritarian character, like that which it has again assumed today in Bolshevism:

> "I am not a communist, because communism unites all the forces of society in the state and becomes absorbed in it; because it inevitably leads to the concentration of all property in the hands of the state, while I seek the complete elimination of the principles of authority and governmental guardianship, which under the pretence of making men

8. Tucker (b1854) published the individualist periodical Liberty

9. Heywood (b1829), abolitionist, feminist individualist

10. Tandy (b1867) advocated "voluntary socialism"

11. Stirner (b1806) was individualism's most well-known exponent. writing *The Ego and His Own*

12. Bakunin (b1814) is often cited as the founder of modern class-struggle anarchism, clashing with Karl Marx in the First International (see note on p24) before his explusion in 1872

17

1. Peter Kropotkin (1842-1921) was a polymath whose work in evolutionary biology, geography and political philosophy was some of the most celebrated of the 19th and early 20th centuries. He is credited as a founding father of anarchist-communism

moral and civilising them, has up to now always enslaved, oppressed, exploited and ruined them."

Bakunin was a determined revolutionary and did not believe in an amicable adjustment of the existing conflicts within society. He recognised that the ruling classes blindly and stubbornly opposed every possibility for larger social reforms, and accordingly saw the only salvation in an international social revolution, which would abolish all institutions of political power and economic exploitation and introduce in their stead a federation of free associations of producers and consumers to provide for the requirements of their daily life.

Since he, like so many of his contemporaries, believed in the close proximity of the revolution, he directed all his vast energy to combining all the genuinely revolutionary and libertarian elements within and outside the International to safeguard the coming revolution against any dictatorship or any retrogression to the old conditions. Thus he became in a very special sense the creator of the modern anarchist movement.

Anarchism found a valuable exponent in Peter Kropotkin[1], who set himself the task of making the achievements of modern natural science available for the development of the sociological concept of anarchism. In his ingenious book, *Mutual Aid, A Factor of Evolution*, he entered the lists against so-called Social Darwinism, whose exponents tried to prove the inevitability of the existing social conditions from the Darwinian theory of the struggle for existence by raising the struggle of the strong against the weak to the status of an iron law of nature, to which man is also subject.

In reality this conception was strongly influenced by the Malthusian doctrine that life's table is not spread for all, and that the unneeded will just have to reconcile themselves to this fact. Kropotkin showed that this conception of nature as a field of unrestricted warfare is only a caricature of real life, and that along with the brutal struggle for existence, which is fought out with tooth and claw, there exists in nature also another tendency which is expressed in the social combination of the weaker species and the maintenance of races by the evolution of social instincts and mutual aid.

In this sense man is not the creator of society, but society the creator of man, for he inherited from the species that preceded him the social instinct which alone enabled him to maintain himself in his first environment against the physical superiority of other species, and to make sure of an undreamed-of height of development.

This second as is shown by the steady retrogression of those species whose tendency in the struggle for existence is far superior to the first, have no social life and are dependent merely upon their physical strength. This view, which to-day is meeting with constantly wider acceptance in the natural sciences and in social research, opened wholly new vistas to the prospects concerning human evolution.

According to Kropotkin the fact remains that even under the worst despotism most of man's personal relations with his fellows are arranged by social habits, free agreement and mutual cooperation, without which social life would not be possible at all. If this were not the case, even the strongest coercive machinery of the state would not be able to maintain the social order for any length of time.

However these natural forms of behaviour, which arise from man's innermost nature, are to-day constantly interfered with and crippled by the effects of economic exploitation and governmental tutelage, representing the brutal form of the struggle for existence in human society which has to be overcome by the other form of mutual aid and free co-operation. The consciousness of personal responsibility and the capacity for sympathy with others, which make all social ethics and all ideas of social justice, develop best in freedom.

Like Bakunin, Kropotkin too was a revolutionary. But he, like Elisee Reclus[2] and others, saw in revolution only a special phase of the evolutionary process, which appears when new social aspirations are so restricted in their natural development by authority that they have to shatter the old shell by violence before they can function as new factors in human life.

In contrast to Proudhon's mutualism and Bakunin's collectivism, Kropotkin advocated common ownership not only of the means of production but of the products of labour as well, as it was his opinion that in the present state of technology no exact measure of the value of individual labour is possible, but that, on the other hand, by rational direction of our modern methods of labour it will be possible to assure comparative abundance to every human being.

2. Élisée Reclus (1830-1905) was a geographer, conservationist and anarchist philosopher, sometimes hailed as a founding influence of social ecology

1. Joseph Déjacque (1821-1864), a French anarchist-communist poet and theorist who coined the term libertarian. He was a major critic of Proudhon's sexist tendencies and support for individual ownership of labour products

Communist anarchism, which before Kropotkin had already been urged by Joseph Dejacque[1], Elisee Reclus, Carlo Cafiero[2] and others, and which is recognised by the great majority of anarchists today, found in him its most brilliant exponent.

Mention must also be made here of Leo Tolstoy, who, from primitive Christianity and on the basis of the ethical principles laid down in the gospels, arrived at the idea of a society without rulership.

Common to all anarchists is the desire to free society of all political and social coercive institutions which stand in the way of the development of a free humanity. In this sense mutualism, collectivism and communism are not to be regarded as closed economic systems, permitting no further development, but merely as economic assumptions as to the means of safeguarding a free community. There will even probably be in every form of a free society of the future different forms of economic co-operation existing side by side, since any social progress must be associated with free experimentation and practical testing out of new methods for which in a free society of free communities there will be every opportunity.

The same holds true for the various methods of anarchism. The work of its adherents is pre-eminently a work of education to prepare the people intellectually and psychologically for the tasks of their social liberation.

Every attempt to limit the influence of economic monopolism and the power of the state is a step nearer to the realisation of this goal. Every development of voluntary organisation in the various fields of social activity towards the direction of personal freedom and social justice deepens the awareness of the people and strengthens their social responsibility, without which no changes in social life can be accomplished.

Most anarchists of our time are convinced that such a transformation of society will take years of constructive work and education and cannot be brought about without revolutionary convulsions which till now have always accomplished every progress in social life. The character of these convulsions, of course, depends entirely on the strength of resistance with which the ruling classes will be able to oppose the realisation of the new ideas.

The wider the circles which are inspired with the idea of a reorganisation of society in the spirit of freedom and socialism, the easier will be the birth pains of new social changes in the future. For even revolutions can only develop and mature the ideas which already exist and have made their way into the consciousness of men: but they cannot themselves create new ideas or generate new worlds out of nothing.

Before the appearance of totalitarian states in Russia, Italy, Germany and later in Portugal and Spain, and the outbreak of the Second World War, anarchist organisations and movements existed almost in every country. But like all other socialist movements of that period, they became the victims of fascist tyranny and the invasions of the German armies, and could only lead an underground existence.

Since the end of the war a resurrection of anarchist movements in all Western European countries is to be noticed. The federations of the French and Italian anarchists already held their first conventions, and so did the Spanish anarchists of whom many thousands are still living in exile, mostly in France, Belgium and North Africa[3].

Anarchist papers and magazines are published again in many European countries and in North and South America.

2. Carlo Cafiero (1846-1892) was an Italian anarchist and champion of Mikhail Bakunin

3. Rocker is referring to World War Two, but the Spanish exiles were primarily made up of former members of the anarchist CNT union defeated in the Spanish Civil War (1936-39), who would go on to form a core of resistance to Franco over the next three decades of his rule and a focal point for libertarian organising after his death

3. THE ORIGINS OF ANARCHO-SYNDICALISM

any anarchists spent a great part of their activities in the labour movement, especially in the Latin countries, where in later years the movement of anarcho-syndicalism was born. Its theoretical assumptions were based on the teachings of libertarian or anarchist socialism, while its form of organisation was taken from the movement of revolutionary syndicalism which in the years from 1895 to 1910 experienced a marked upswing, particularly in France, Italy and Spain. Its ideas and methods, however, were not new.

They had already found a deep resonance in the ranks of the First International[1] when the great association had reached the zenith of its intellectual development.

This was plainly revealed in the debates at its fourth congress in Basel (1869) concerning the importance of the economic organisations of the workers. In his report upon this question which Eugène Hins[2] laid before the congress in the name of the Belgian Federation, there was presented for the first time a wholly new point of view which had an unmistakable resemblance to certain ideas of Robert Owen and the English labour movement of the 1830s.

In order to make a correct estimate of this, one must remember that at that time the various schools of state-socialism attributed no, or at best, only little importance, to the trade unions. The French Blanquists[3] saw in these organisations merely a reform movement, with a socialist dictatorship as their immediate aim.

Ferdinand Lassalle[4] and his followers directed all their activities towards welding the workers into a political party and were outspoken opponents of all trade union endeavours in which they saw only a hindrance to the political evolution of the working class.

Marx and his adherents of that period recognised, it is true, the necessity of trade unions for the achievement of certain betterments within the capitalist system, but they believed that their role would be exhausted with this, and that they would disappear along with capitalism, since the transition

1. The First International (1864–1876) was an organisation which aimed to bring socialist, anarchist and Marxist currents across Europe under one banner. After extraordinary initial success, it sunk under the weight of the divisions in its ranks, most famously between the anarchists, led by Mikhail Bakunin, and the followers of Karl Marx

2. Eugène Hins (1839-1923) was an influential freethinker, positivist and founder of the Belgian section of the First International who backed Bakunin during the disputes

to socialism could be guided only by a proletarian dictatorship.

In Basel this idea underwent for the first time a thorough critical examination. The views expressed in the Belgian report presented by Hins which were shared by the delegates from Spain, the Swiss Jura and the larger part of the French sections were based on the premise that the present economic associations of the workers are not only a necessity within the present society, but were even more to be regarded as the social nucleus of a coming socialist economy, and it was, therefore, the duty of the International to educate the workers for this task. In accordance with this the congress adopted the following resolution:

> "The congress declares that all workers should strive to establish associations for resistance in their various trades. As soon as a trade union is formed the unions in the same trade are to be notified so that the formation of national alliances in the industries may begin.
>
> "These alliances shall be charged with the duty of collecting all material relating to their industry, of advising about measures to be executed in common, and of seeing that they are carried out, to the end that the present wage system may be replaced by the federation of free producers. The congress directs the General Council to provide for the alliance of the trade unions of all countries."

In his argument for the resolution proposed by the committee, Hins explained that "by this dual form of organisation of local workers' associations and general alliances for each industry on the one hand and the political administration of labour councils on the other, the general representation of labour, regional, national and international, will be provided for. The councils of the trades and industrial organisations will take the place of the present government, and this representation of labour will do away, once and forever, with the governments of the past."

This new idea grew out of the recognition that every new economic form of society must be accompanied by a new political form of the social organism and could only attain practical expression in this. Its followers saw in the present national

3. Blanquism, named for Louis Blanqui, advocated the seizure of power by a group of organised conspirators who would then implement socialism. At the time of writing it was sometimes used as an insult aimed at Marxists to illustrate the folly of mixing up the needs of a Party with those of the people

4. Lassalle (1825–64) helped popularise a number of social democratic and internationalist ideas in Germany

5. The Jura Federation was an influential early anarchist group based in the watchmaking community in Switzerland

23

1. The Paris Commune (1871) represented the first working class capture of a major city of the industrial age. The brutal crushing of the rebels by the army of Versailles and subsequent execution of 20,000 people after two months of self-governance was a pivotal moment which seriously undermined the class struggle movement of the time

state only the political agent and defender of the possessing classes, and did, therefore, not strive for the conquest of power, but for the elimination of every system of power within society, in which they saw the requisite preliminary condition for all tyranny and exploitation.

They understood that along with the monopoly of property, the monopoly of power must also disappear. Proceeding from their recognition that the lordship of man over man had had its day, they sought to familiarise themselves with the administration of things. Or as Bakunin, one of the great forerunners of modern anarcho-syndicalism, put it:

"Since the organisation of the International has as its goal, not the setting up of new states or despots, but the radical elimination of every separate sovereignty, it must have an essentially different character from the organisation of the state.

"To just the degree that the latter is authoritarian, artificial and violent, alien and hostile to the natural development of the interests and the instincts of the people, to the same degree must the organisation of the International be free, natural and in every respect in accord with those interests and instincts.

"But what is the natural organisation of the masses? It is one based on the different occupations of their actual daily life, on their various kinds of work, organisation according to their occupations, trade organisations.

"When all industries, including the various branches of agriculture, are represented in the International, its organisation, the organisation of the toiling masses of the people, will be finished."

And at another occasion:

"All this practical and vital study of social science by the workers themselves in their trades sections and their chambers of labour will – and already has – engender in them the unanimous, well-considered, theoretically and practically demonstrable conviction that the serious, final complete liberation of the workers is possible only on one condition: that of the appropriation of capital, that is, of raw materials and all the tools of labour, including land, by the whole body of the workers ...

"The organisation of the trade sections, their federation in the International, and their representation by the Labour Chambers, not only create a great academy in which the workers of the International, combining theory and practice, can and must study economic science, they also bear in themselves the living germs of the new social order, which is to replace the bourgeois world. They are creating not only the ideas but also the facts of the future itself."

After the decline of the International and the Franco-German War, by which the focal point of the socialist labour movement was transferred to Germany, whose workers had neither revolutionary traditions nor that rich experience possessed by the socialists in the Western countries, those ideas were gradually forgotten.

After the defeat of the Paris Commune[1] and the revolutionary upheavals in Spain and Italy[2] the sections of the International in these countries were compelled for many years to carry on only an underground existence. Only with the awakening of revolutionary syndicalism in France were the ideas of the First International rescued from oblivion and inspired once more larger sections of the labour movement.

4. SOCIALISM AND ANARCHO-SYNDICALISM IN FRANCE

1. The Federation des Bourse du Travail was a French socialist-backed institution which ran buildings and services for training, employment and political education nationwide. Their political heyday was from 1897 to the 1920s

2. Georges Sorel (1847-1922), founder of the theory and "social myth" and "virtue of violence"

3. Edouard Berth (1875-1939) argued a strict form of "produuctivist" syndicalism to "out-capitalist" the capitalists

4. Hubert Lagardelle (1874-1958), influential early writer but drifted right, ending up as a Vichy government minister

5. The Allemanists were a union-centric party strongly linked to the Marxists

**odern** anarcho-syndicalism is a direct continuation of those social aspirations which took shape in the bosom of the First International and which were best understood and most strongly held by the libertarian wing of the great workers' alliance.

Its development was a direct reaction against the concepts and methods of political socialism, a reaction which in the decade before the First World War had already manifested itself in the strong upsurge of the anarcho-syndicalist movement in France, Italy and especially Spain, where the great majority of the organised workers had always remained faithful to the doctrines of the libertarian wing of the International.

It was in France that the opposition against the ideas and methods of the modern labour parties found a clear expression in the theories and tactics of revolutionary syndicalism. The immediate cause for the development of these new tendencies in the French labour movement was the continual split of the various socialist parties in France. All these parties, with the exception of the Allemanists, which later gave up parliamentary activities completely, saw in the trade unions merely recruiting schools for their political objectives and had no understanding for their real functions. The constant dissensions among the various socialist factions was naturally carried over into the labour unions, and it happened quite frequently that when the unions of one faction went on strike the unions of the other factions walked in on them as strike breakers.

This untenable situation gradually opened the eyes of the workers. So the trade union congress in Nantes (1894) charged a special committee with the task of devising means for bringing about an understanding among all the trade union alliances. The result was the founding in the following year of the Confederation Generale du Travail (CGT) at the congress in Limoges, which declared itself independent of all political parties. From then on there existed in France only two large trade union groups, the CGT and the Federation des Bourses du Travail[1], and in 1902, at the congress of the Montpellier the latter joined the CGT.

One often encounters the widely disseminated opinion, which was fostered by Werner Sombart in particular, that revolutionary syndicalism in France owes its origin to intellectuals like G Sorel[2], E Berth[3] and H Lagardelle[4], who in the periodical *Le Mouvement Socialiste*, founded in 1899, elaborated in their way the intellectual results of the new movement.

This is utterly false. None of these men belonged to the movement, nor had they any appreciable influence in its internal development. Moreover, the CGT was not composed exclusively of revolutionary syndicates; certainly half of its members were of reformist tendency and had joined the CGT because even they recognised that the dependence of the trade unions on political parties was a misfortune for the movement.

But the revolutionary wing, which had had the most energetic and active elements of organised labour on its side as well as the most brilliant intellectual forces in the organisation, gave the CGT its characteristic stamp, and it was they who determined the development of the ideas of revolutionary syndicalism.

Many of them came from the Allemanists[5], but even more from the ranks of the anarchists, like Fernand Pelloutier[6], the highly intelligent secretary of the Bourse du Travaille, Emile Pouget[7], the editor of the official organ of the CGT *La Voix du Peuple*, P. Delesalle[8], G. Yvetot[9] and many others. It was mainly under the influence of the radical wing of the CGT that the new movement developed and found its expression in the Charter of Amiens (1906), in which the principles and methods of the movement were laid down.

This new movement in France found a strong echo among the Latin workers and penetrated also into other countries. The influence of French syndicalism at that time on larger and smaller sections of the international labour movement was strengthened in great degree by the internal crisis which at that period infected nearly all the socialist labour parties in Europe.

The battle between the so-called Revisionists[10] and the rigid Marxists, and particularly the fact that their very parliamentary activities forced the most violent opponents of the evisionists of natural necessity to travel along the path of revisionism,

6. Pelloutier (1867-1901), major influence on Sorel and the emergence of Italian Revolutionaay Syndicalism

7. Pouget (1860-1931), founding thinker of anarcho-syndicalism and helped popularise sabotage as a method of workplace dissent

8. Paul Delesalle (1870-1948), former steel worker, core anarchist militant and Pouget's biographer

9. Georges Yvetot (1868-1942), ally of Pelloutier and succeeded him as secretary of the Bourse du Travail

10. Revisionists sat within the broad socialist movement, but argued for it to be achieved through democratic "evolutionary" means

caused many of the more thoughtful elements to reflect seriously.

They realised that participation in the politics of the nationalist states had not brought the labour movement a hair-breadth nearer to socialism, but had helped greatly to destroy the belief in the necessity of constructive socialist activity, and, worst of all, had robbed the people of their initiative by giving them the ruinous delusion that salvation always comes from above.

Under these circumstances socialism steadily lost its character of a cultural ideal, which was to prepare the workers for the dissolution of the present capitalist system and, therefore, could not let itself be halted by the artificial frontiers of the national states.

In the mind of the leaders of the modern labour parties the alleged aims of their movement were more and more blended with the interests of the national state, until at last they became unable to distinguish any definite boundary whatever between them.

It would be a mistake to find in this strange about-face an intentional betrayal by the leaders, as has so often been asserted. The truth is that we have to do here with a gradual assimilation to the modes and thoughts of the present society which necessarily had to affect the intellectual attitude of the leaders of the various labour parties in every country.

Those very parties which had once set out to conquer political power under the flag of socialism saw themselves compelled by the iron logic of conditions to sacrifice their socialist convictions bit by bit to the national policies of the state. The political power which they had wanted to conquer had gradually conquered their socialism until there was scarcely anything left but the name.

5. THE ROLE OF THE TRADE UNIONS: ANARCHO-SYNDICALIST VIEW

These were the considerations which led to the development of revolutionary syndicalism or, as it was later called, anarcho-syndicalism in France and other countries. The term workers' syndicate meant at first merely an organisation of producers for the immediate betterment of their economic and social status. But the rise of revolutionary syndicalism gave this original meaning a much wider and deeper import.

Just as the party is a unified organisation, with definite political effort within the modern constitutional state which seeks to maintain the present order of society in one form or another, so, according to the unionist's view, the trade unions are the unified organisation of labour and have for their purpose the defence of the producers within existing society and the preparing for and practical carrying out of the reconstruction of social life in the direction of socialism. They have, therefore, a double purpose:

> **1.** To enforce the demands of the producers for the safeguarding and raising of their standard of living;
> **2.** To acquaint the workers with the technical management of production and economic life in general and prepare them to take the socio-economic organism into their own hands and shape it according to socialist principles.

Anarcho-syndicalists are of the opinion that political parties are not fitted to perform either of these two tasks. According to their conceptions the trade union has to be the spearhead of the labour movement, toughened by daily combats and permeated by a socialist spirit. Only in the realm of economy are workers able to display their full strength; for it is their activity as producers which holds together the social structure and guarantees the existence of society.

Only as a producer and creator of social wealth does the worker become aware of his strength. In solidary union with his followers he creates the great phalanx of militant labour, aflame with the spirit of freedom and animated by the ideal of social justice. For the anarcho-syndicalists the labour syndicate are the most fruitful germs of a future society, the elementary school of socialism in general. Every new social structure creates organs for itself in the body of the old organism; without this prerequisite every social evolution is unthinkable.

To them socialist education does not mean participation in the power policy of the national state, but the effort to make clear to the workers the intrinsic connections among social problems by technical instruction and the development of their administrative capacities, to prepare them for their role of re-shapers of economic life and give them the moral assurance required for the performance of their task.

No social body is better fitted for this purpose than the economic fighting organisation of the workers; it gives a definite direction to their social activities and toughens their resistance in the immediate struggle for the necessities of life and the defence of their human rights. At the same time it develops their ethical concepts without which any social transformation is impossible: vital solidarity with their fellows in destiny and moral responsibility for their actions.

Just because the educational work of anarcho-syndicalists is directed toward the development of independent thought and action, they are outspoken opponents of all centralising tendencies which are so characteristic of most of the present labour parties. Centralism, that artificial scheme which operates from the top towards the bottom and turns over the affairs of administration to a small minority, is always attended by barren official routine; it crushes individual conviction, kills all personal initiative by lifeless discipline and bureaucratic ossification.

For the state, centralism is the appropriate form of organisation, since it aims at the greatest possible uniformity of social life for the maintenance of political and social equilibrium. But for a movement whose very existence depends on prompt action at any favourable moment and on the independent thought of its supporters, centralism is a curse which weakens its power of decision and systematically represses every spontaneous initiative.

The organisation of anarcho-syndicalism is based upon the principles of federalism, on free combination from below upward, putting the right of self-determination of every union above everything else and recognising only the organic agreement of all on the basis of like interests and common conviction. Their organisation is accordingly constructed on the following basis: The workers in each locality join the unions of their respective trades. The trade unions of a city or a rural district combine in Labour Chambers which constitute the centres for local propaganda and education, and weld the workers together as producers to prevent the rise of any narrow-minded factional spirit. In times of local labour troubles they arrange for the united co-operation of the whole body of locally organised labour.

All the Labour Chambers are grouped according to districts and regions to form the National Federation of Labour Chambers, which maintains the permanent connection among the local bodies, arranges free adjustment of the productive labour of the members of the various organisations on; co-operative lines, provides for the necessary co-ordination in the work of education and supports the local groups with council and guidance.

Every trade union is, moreover, federatively allied with all the organisations of the same industry, and these in turn with all related trades, so that all are combined in general industrial and agricultural alliances. It is their task to meet the demands of the daily struggles between capital and labour and to combine all the forces of the movement for common action where the; necessity arises. Thus the Federation of the Labour Chambers and the Federation of the Industrial Alliances constitute the two poles about which the whole life of the labour syndicates revolves.

Such a form of organisation not only gives the workers every opportunity for direct action in the struggle for their daily bread, but it also provides them with the necessary preliminaries for the reorganisation of society, their own strength, and without alien intervention in case of a revolutionary crisis.

Anarcho-syndicalists are convinced that a socialist economic order cannot be created by the decrees and statutes of any government, but only by the unqualified collaboration of the workers, technicians and peasants to carry on production and distribution by their own administration in the interest of the community and on the basis of mutual agreements.

In such a situation the Labour Chambers would take over the administration of existing social capital in each community, determine the needs of the inhabitants of their districts and organise local consumption. Through the agency of the Federation of Labour Chambers it would be possible to calculate the total requirements of the whole country and adjust the work of production accordingly. On the other hand it would be the task of the Industrial and Agricultural Alliances to take control of the instruments of production, transportation, etc, and provide the separate producing groups with what they need. In a word:

> **1.** Organisation of the total production of the country by the Federation of the Industrial Alliances and direction of work by labour councils elected by the workers themselves;
> **2.** Organisation of social contribution by the Federation of the Labour Chambers.

In this respect, also, practical experience has given the best instruction. It has shown that the many problems of a socialist reconstruction of society cannot be solved by any government, even when the famous dictatorship of the proletariat is meant. In Russia the Bolshevist dictatorship[1] stood helpless for almost two years before the economic problems and tried to hide its incapacity behind a flood of decrees and ordinances most of which were buried at once in the various bureaus. If the world could be set free by decrees, there would long ago have been no problems left in Russia.

In its fanatical zeal for power, Bolshevism has violently destroyed the most valuable organs of a socialist order, by suppressing the Co-operative Societies, bringing the trade unions under state control, and depriving the Soviets of their independence almost from the beginning.

So the dictatorship of the proletariat paved the way not for a socialist society but for the most primitive type of bureaucratic state capitalism and a reversion to political absolutism which was long ago abolished in most countries by bourgeois revolutions. In his *Message to the Workers of the West European Countries* Kropotkin said, rightfully:

> "Russia has shown us the way in which socialism cannot be realised, although the people, nauseated with the old regime, expressed no active resistance to the experiments of the new government.
> "The idea of workers' councils for the control of the political and economic life of the country is, in itself, of extraordinary importance ... but so long as the country is dominated by the dictatorship of a party, the workers' and peasants' councils naturally lose their significance.
> "They are hereby degraded to the same passive role which the representatives of the estates used to play in the time of the absolute monarchy."

6. THE STRUGGLE IN GERMANY AND SPAIN

In Germany, however, where the moderate wing of political socialism had attained power[1], socialism, in its long years of absorption with routine parliamentary tasks, had become so bogged down that it was no longer capable of any creative action whatever.

Even a bourgeois paper like the *Frankfurter Zeitung* felt obliged to confirm that "the history of European peoples had not previously produced a revolution that has been so poor in creative ideas and so weak in revolutionary energy." The mere fact that a party with a larger membership than any other of the various labour parties in the world, which was for many years the strongest political body in Germany, had to leave the field to Hitler and his gang without any resistance speaks for itself and presents an example of helplessness and weakness which can hardly be misunderstood.

One has only to compare the German situation of those days with the attitude of the anarcho-syndicalist labour unions in Spain and especially in Catalonia, where their influence was strongest, to realise the whole difference between the labour movement of these two countries. When in July, 1936 the conspiracy of the fascist army leaders ripened into open revolt, it was by the heroic resistance of the National Federation of Labour (CNT) and the Anarchist Federation of Iberia (FAI)[2] that the fascist uprising in Catalonia was put down within a few days, ridding this most important part of Spain of the enemy and frustrating the original plan of the conspirators to take Barcelona by surprise.

The workers could then not stop half-way; so there followed the collectivisation of the land and the taking over of the plants by the workers' and peasants' syndicates. This movement, which was released by the initiative of the CNT and FAI with irresistible power, overran Aragon, the Levante and other sections of the country and even swept along with it a large part of the unions of the socialist Party in the General Labour Union (UGT).

This event revealed that the anarcho-syndicalist workers of Spain not only knew how to fight, but that they were also filled with the constructive ideas which are so necessary in the time of a real crisis.

1. Rocker is referring here to the period shortly after World War One, which saw parliament dominated by Friedrich Ebert's Social Democrats

2. The CNT was the largest anarchist union ever created, claiming a membership of up to 3 million people at its height. The FAI was a grouping within the wider CNT which was formed to prevent it sliding into bureaucracy or rightwards and exercised a considerable level of control during the Civil War – though prominent FAI figures would later take senior government posts

It is to the great merit of libertarian socialism in Spain that since the time of the First International it has trained the workers in that spirit which treasures freedom above all else and regards the intellectual independence of its adherents as the basis of its existence.

It was the passive and lifeless attitude of the organised workers in other countries, who put up with the policy of non-intervention of their governments that led to the defeat of the Spanish workers and peasants after a heroic struggle of more than two and one half years.

7. THE POLITICAL STRUGGLE: ANARCHO-SYNDICALIST VIEW

It has often been charged against anarcho-syndicalism that its adherents had no interest in the political structure of the different countries and consequently no interest in the political struggles of the time. This idea is altogether erroneous and springs either from outright ignorance or wilful distortion of the facts. It is not the political struggle as such which distinguishes the revolutionary unionists from the modern labour parties, both in principles and tactics. but the form of this struggle and the aims which it has in view.

Anarcho-syndicalists pursue the same tactics in their fight against political suppression as against economic exploitation. But while they are convinced that along with the system of exploitation its political protective device, the state, will also disappear to give place to the administration of public affairs on the basis of free agreement, they do not at all overlook the fact that the efforts of organised labour within the existing political and social order must always be directed against any attack of reaction, and constantly widening the scope of these rights wherever the opportunity for this presents itself. The heroic struggle of the CNT in Spain against fascism was, perhaps, the best proof that the alleged non-political attitude of the anarcho-syndicalists is but idle talk.

But according to their opinion the point of attack in the political struggle lies not in the legislative bodies but in the people.

Political rights do not originate in parliaments; they are rather forced upon them from without. And even their enactment into; law has for a long time been no guarantee of their security. They do not exist because they have been legally set down on a piece of paper, but only when they have become the ingrown habit of a people, and when any attempt to impair them will meet with the violent resistance of the populace.

Where this is not the case, there is no help in any parliamentary opposition or any Platonic appeals to the constitution. One compels respect from others when one knows how to defend one's dignity as a human being. This is not only true in private life; it has always been the same in political life as well.

All political rights and liberties which people enjoy to-day, they do not owe to the good will of their governments, but to their own strength. Governments have always employed every means in their power to prevent the attainment of these rights or render them illusory. Great mass movements and whole revolutions have been necessary to wrest them from the ruling classes, who would never have consented to them voluntarily. The whole history of the last three hundred years is proof of that.

What is important is not that governments have decided to concede certain rights to the people, but the reason why they had to do this. Of course, if one accepts Lenin's cynical phrase and thinks of freedom merely as a "bourgeois prejudice", then, to be sure, political rights have no value at all for the workers. But then the countless struggles of the past, all the revolts and revolutions to which we owe these rights, are also without value. To proclaim this bit of wisdom it hardly was necessary to overthrow Tzarism, for even the censorship of Nicholas II would certainly have had no objection to the designation of freedom as a bourgeois prejudice.

If anarcho-syndicalism nevertheless rejects the participation in the present national parliaments, it is not because they have no sympathy with political struggles in general, but because its adherents are of the opinion that this form of activity is the very weakest and most helpless form of the political struggle for the workers.

For the possessing classes, parliamentary action is certainly an appropriate instrument for the settlement of such conflicts as arise, because they are all equally interested in maintaining the present economic and social order. Where there is a common interest mutual agreement is possible and serviceable to all parties. But for the workers the situation is very different.

For them the existing economic order is the source of their exploitation and their social and political subjugation. Even the freest ballot cannot do away with the glaring contrast between the possessing and non-possessing classes in society. It can only give the servitude of the toiling masses the stamp of legality.

It is a fact that when socialist labour parties have wanted to achieve some decisive political reforms they could not do it by parliamentary action, but were obliged to rely wholly on the economic fighting power of the workers. The political general strikes in

Belgium and Sweden for the attainment of universal suffrage are proof of this.

And in Russia it was the great general strike in 1905[1] that forced the Tsar to sign the new constitution. It was the recognition of this which impelled the anarcho-syndicalists to centre their activity on the socialist education of the masses and the utilisation of their economic and social power. Their method is that of direct action in both the economic and political struggle of the time. By direct action they mean every method of the immediate struggle by the workers against economic and political oppression. Among these the outstanding are the strike in all its gradations, from the simple wage struggle to the general strike, organised boycott and all the other countless means which workers as producers have in their hands.

One of the most effective forms of direct action is the social strike, which was hitherto mostly used in Spain and partly in France, and which shows a remarkable and growing responsibility of the workers to society as a whole.

It is less concerned with the immediate interests of the producers than with the protection of the community against the most pernicious outgrowths of the present system. The social strike seeks to force upon the employers a responsibility to the public. Primarily it has in view the protection of the consumers, of which the workers themselves constitute the great majority.

Under the present circumstances the workers are frequently debased by doing a thousand things which constantly serve only to injure the whole community for the advantage of the employers. They are compelled to make use of inferior and often actually injurious materials in the fabrication of their products, to erect wretched dwellings, to put up spoiled foodstuffs and to perpetrate innumerable acts that are planned to cheat the consumer. To interfere vigorously is, in the opinion of the anarcho-syndicalists, the great task of the labour syndicates.

An advance in this direction would at the same time enhance the position of the workers in society, and in larger measure confirm that position.

Direct action by organised labour finds its strongest expression in the general strike, in the stoppage of work in every branch of production in cases where every other means is failing. It is the most powerful weapon which the workers have at their command and gives the most comprehensive expression to their strength as a social factor.

1. The 1905 revolution was spread across most of the Russian Empire and was only brough to a halt after the monarchy made significant concessions, most famously the limiting of monarchichal power and the establishment of a state parliament, the Duma

1. The 1902 Barcelona strike saw 80,000 people walk out and such widespread insurrectionary activity that martial law was declared

The general strike, of course, is not an agency that can be invoked arbitrarily on every occasion. It needs certain social assumptions to give it a proper moral strength and make it a proclamation of the will of the broad masses of the people. The ridiculous claim, which is so often attributed to the revolutionary unionists, that it is only necessary to proclaim a general strike in order to achieve a socialist society in a few days, is, of course just a ludicrous invention of ignorant opponents. The general strike can serve various purposes.

It can be the last stage of a sympathetic strike, as. for example, in Barcelona in 1902[1] or in Bilbao in 1903, which enabled the miners to get rid of the hated truck system and compelled the employers to establish sanitary conditions in the mines. It can also be a means of organised labour to enforce some general demand, as, for example, in the attempted general strike in the USA in 1886, to compel the granting of the eight-hour day in ail industries. The great general strike of the English workers in 1926 was the result of a planned attempt by the employers to lower the general standard of living of the workers by a cut in wages.

But the general strike can also have political objectives in view. as, for example, the fight of the Spanish workers in 1904 for the liberation of political prisoners, or the general strike in Catalonia in July 1909, to force the government to terminate its criminal war in Morocco. Also the general strike of the German workers in 1920, which was instituted after the so-called Kapp putsch and put an end to a government that had attained power by a military uprising, belongs to this category.

In such critical situations the general strike takes the place of the barricades of the political uprisings of the past. For the workers, the general strike is the logical outcome of the modern industrial system, whose victims they are to-day, and at the same time it offers them their strongest weapon in the struggle for their social liberation, provided they recognise their own strength and learn how to use this weapon properly.

8. ANARCHO-SYNDICALISM SINCE THE FIRST WORLD WAR

After the First World War the peoples in Europe faced a new situation. In Central Europe the old regime had collapsed. Russia found herself in the midst of a social revolution of which no one could see the end. The Russian revolution had impressed the workers of every country very deeply.

They felt that Europe was in the midst of a revolutionary crisis and that if nothing decisive came out of it now their hopes would be dispelled for many years For this reason they based the highest hopes on the Russian Revolution and saw in it the inauguration of a new era in European history. In 1919, the Bolshevist party, which had attained power in Russia, issued an appeal to all the revolutionary workers organisations of the world and invited them to a congress in the following year in Moscow to set up a new International.

Communist parties at this time existed only in a few countries; on the other hand there were in Spain. Portugal, France, Italy, Holland, Sweden, Germany, England and the countries of North and South America unionist organisations, some of which exercised a very strong influence. It was, therefore, the deep concern of Lenin and his followers to win these particular organisations for their purpose. So it came about that at the congress for the founding of the Third International[2] in the summer of 1920 almost all the anarcho-syndicalists of Europe were represented.

But the impression which the revolutionary unionist delegates received in Russia was not calculated to make them regard collaboration with the communists as either possible or desirable. The dictatorship of the proletariat[3] was already revealing itself in its true light.

The prisons were filled with socialists of every school, among them many anarchists and unionists. But above all it was plain that the new dominant caste was in no way fitted for the task of a genuine socialist construction of life. The foundation of the Third International with its dictatorial apparatus and its efforts to make the whole labour movement in Europe into an instrument for the foreign policy of the Bolshevist state, quickly made plain to the revolutionary unionist that there was no place for them in the Third International.

For this reason the congress in Moscow decided

2. The Third International (1919–1943), also known as the Comintern, attempted to bring all the socialist forces of Europe under the banner of the Soviet Union

3. The dictatorship of the proletariat is a Marxist term denoting the total control of society by the working classes and forcible dismantling of the apparatus and assets of other classes. In practice, this has often been conflated with the Leninist idea that what's good for the Party is what's good for the proletariat, thus justifying the dictatorship of the Party

1. The Profintern (1921-1937), also known as the Red Trade Union International, was the USSR-backed sibling of the more party-oriented Comintern

to set up alongside the Third International a separate international alliance of revolutionary trade unions[1], in which the unionist organisations of all shades could also find a place. The unionist delegates agreed to this proposal, but when the communists demanded that this new organisation should be subordinate to the Third International, this demand was unanimously rejected by the anarcho-syndicalists.

In December, 1920 an international anarcho-syndicalist conference convened in Berlin to decide upon an attitude toward the approaching congress of the Red Trade Union International, which was prepared in Moscow for the following year. The conference agreed upon seven points on whose acceptance the entrance of the unionists in that body was made dependent. The importance of those seven points was the complete independence of the movement from all political parties, and insistence on the viewpoint that the socialist reconstruction of society could only be carried out by the economic organisations of the producing classes themselves. At the congress in Moscow in the following year the unionist organisations were in the minority.

The Central Alliance of Russian Trade Unions dominated the entire situation and put through all the resolutions. In October, 1921, an international conference of unionists was held in Dusseldorf, Germany, and it decided to call an international convention in Berlin during the following year. This convention met from December 25, 1922 until January 2, 1923. The following organisations were represented.

Argentina by the Federacion Obrera Regional Argentina, with 200,000 members;
Chile by the Industrial Workers of the World with 20,000 members;
Denmark by the Union for Unionist Propaganda with 600 members;
Germany by the Freie Arbeiter Union with 120,000 members
Holland by the National Arbeids Sekretariat with 22,500 members,
Italy by the Unione Sindicale Italiana with 500,000 members;
Mexico by the Confederacion General de Trabajadores,
Norway by the Norsk Syndikalistik Federasjon with 20,000 members;
Portugal by the Confederacao Geral do

Trabalho with 150,000 members;
Sweden by the Sveriges Arbetares Centralorganisation with 32,000 members.

The **Spanish** CNT at that time was engaged in a terrific struggle against the dictatorship of Primo de Rivera and had sent no delegates, but they re-affirmed their adherence at the secret congress in Saragossa in October, 1923.

In **France**, where after the war a split in the CGT had led to the founding of the CGTU, the latter had already joined Moscow. But there was a minority in the organisation which had combined to form the Comite de Defence Unioniste Revolutionaire, representing about 100,000 workers, which took part in the proceedings of the Berlin congress.

From Paris the Federation du Batiment with 32,000 members and the Federation des Jeunesses de la Seine were likewise represented.

Two delegates represented the Unionist Minority of the **Russian** workers.

2. The International Workingmen's Association still exists today, in the form of the International Workers' Association (www.iwa-ait.org)

The congress resolved unanimously on the founding of an international alliance of all unionist organisations under the name International Workingmen's Association[2]. It adopted a declaration of principles which presented an outspoken profession of anarcho-syndicalism. The second item in this declaration runs as follows,

> "Revolutionary syndicalism is the confirmed opponent of every form of economic and social monopoly, and aims at the establishment of free communities and administrative organs of the field and factory workers on the basis of a free system of labour councils, entirely liberated from subordination to any government and parties.
> "Against the politics of the state and political parties it proposes the economic organisation of labour; against the government of men it sets the management of things.
> "Consequently, it has for its object, not the conquest of power, but the abolition of every state function in social life.
> "It believes that, along with the monopoly of property, should also disappear the monopoly of domination, and that any form of the state, including the dictatorship of the proletariat,

1. The Red Week in June came amid a rising number of strikes and riots across Italy and was sparked by the state murder of three anti-militarist protesters in the east coast city of Ancona. Anarchists including Errico Malatesta (pictured) attempted to organise a general revolt against the government but were headed off when the general confederation of labour called off their strike actions

will always be the creator of new monopolies and new privileges, and never an instrument of liberation."

With this the breach with Bolshevism and its adherents in the various countries was completed. The IWMA from then on travelled its own road, held its own international congresses, issued its bulletins and adjusted the relations among the anarcho-syndicalists of the different countries.

The most powerful and influential organisation in the IWMA was the Spanish CNT, the soul of all the hard labour struggles in Spain and later the backbone of the resistance against fascism and the social reorganisation of the country. Before the triumph of Franco, the CNT embraced a membership of about two millions of industrial workers, peasants and intellectual workers.

It controlled 36 daily papers, among them *Solidaridad Obrera* in Barcelona, with a circulation of 240,000, the largest of any paper in Spain, and Castilla Libre, which was the most widely read paper in Madrid. The CNT has published millions of books and pamphlets and contributed more to the education of the masses than any other movement in Spain.

In Portugal the Confederacao Geral do Trabalho, (CGT) founded in 1911, was the strongest labour organisation in the country, and based on the same principles as the CNT in Spain. After the victory of dictatorship, the CGT was forced out of public activity and could only lead an underground existence.

In Italy, under the influence of the ideas of French syndicalism, the anarcho-syndicalist wing of the Conlederazione del Lavoro left that organisation on account of its subservience to the Socialist Party and formed the Unione Sindacale Italiana (USI).

This group was the soul of a long list of severe labour struggles and played a prominent part in the occurrences of the so-called Red Week in June[1], 1914, and later in the occupation of the factories in Milan and other cities in Northern Italy. With the reign of fascism the whole Italian labour movement disappeared along with the USI.

In France the anarcho-syndicalists left the CGTU in 1922, after that organisation yielded entirely to the influence of the Bolshevists, and formed the Confederation Generale du Travail Syndicaliste Revolutionaire, which joined the IWMA.

In Germany there existed for a long time before

the first world war the so-called localists whose stronghold was the Freie Vereinigung deutscher Gewerkschaften (FVDG), founded in 1897. This organisation was originally inspired by social democratic ideas, but it combated the centralising tendencies of the German Trade movement.

The revival of French syndicalism had a great influence on the FVDG and led to its adoption of pure anarcho-syndicalist principles. At its congress in Dusseldorf, 1920, the organisation changed its name to Freie Arbeiter-Union Deutschlands (FAUD).

This movement rendered a great service through the tireless labours of its active publishing house in Berlin which printed a large number of valuable works. After Hitler's accession to power the movement of the FAUD vanished from the scene. A great many of its supporters languished in the concentration camps or had to take refuge abroad.

In Sweden there still exists a very active unionist movement, the Sveriges Arbetares Centralorganisation (SAC), the only unionist organisation in Europe which escaped the reaction of fascism and German invasion during the war.

The Swedish anarcho-syndicalists participated in all the great labour struggles in their country and carried on for many years the work of socialist and libertarian education.

In Holland the anarcho-syndicalist movement concentrated in the Nationale Arbeids Secretariat; but when this organisation came steadily under increasing communist influence, nearly half of its members split off and formed the Nederlandisok Syndikalistisch Vakverbond which joined the IWMA.

In addition to these organisations there were anarcho-syndicalist propaganda groups in Norway, Poland and Bulgaria, which were affiliated with the IWMA The Japanese Jiyu Rengo Dantal Zenkoku Kaigi also joined the ranks of the IWMA

In Argentina the Federacion Obrera Regional Argentina (FORA), founded in 1891, was for many years the centre of most of the big labour struggles in that country. Its history is one of the most tempestuous chapters in the annals of the labour movement.

The movement ran a daily organ, La Protesta, for over 25 years and quite a number of weekly papers all over the country. After the coup d'etat of General Uriburu, the FORA was suppressed, but it carried on underground activity, as it also did under Peron.

In May 1929 the FORA summoned a congress

of all the South American countries to meet in Buenos Aires. At this congress, besides the FORA of Argentina there were represented: Paraguay by the Centro Obrero del Paraguay: Bolivia by the Federacion Local de la Paz, La Antorcha and Luz y Libertad; Mexico by the Confederacion General de Trabajo; Guatemala by the Comite pro Accion Sindical; Uruguay by the Federacion Regional Uruguaya. Brazil was represented by trade unions from seven of the constituent states. Costa Rica was represented by the organisation Hacia la Libertad.

At this congress the Continental American Workingmen's Association was brought into existence, constituting the American division of the IWMA. The seat of this organisation was at first at Buenos Aires, but later, because of the dictatorship, it had to be transferred to Uruguay.

These were the forces which anarcho-syndicalism had at its disposal in the various countries before the reign of fascism and the outbreak of the Second World War.